DON'T TREAD ON THE BUTTERFLIES

Grandfather Sam Wordingham with his first wife, Elizabeth, and their three oldest children, Daisy, Margery, and Sam in 1886

'Don't tread on the butterflies'

memoirs of a childhood
in Heacham and Stiffkey
1912-1932

Joan Sternberg

⚛

with illustrations by
Philippa Abrahams

Larks Press

Published by
The Larks Press
Ordnance Farmhouse, Guist Bottom,
Dereham, Norfolk NR20 5PF

01328 829207

Printed by the Lanceni Press,
Garrood Drive, Fakenham

2000

British Library Cataloguing in Publication Data
A catalogue record for this book is available
from the British Library

THE ARTIST
Philippa Abrahams lives and works in London. She is a graduate of the
Slade School of Fine Art and the Courtauld. Her work is in public and private
collections in England, U.S.A., Canada and Italy. She is also a well-known
expert in the techniques of old master painting and drawing.

ISBN 0 948400 94 3

Heacham 1912-16

The loss of the Titanic was still making headlines in the newspapers when I was born in October 1912 in Heacham, a sizeable village next to Hunstanton on the west coast of Norfolk. The Archduke Ferdinand of Austria-Hungary, whose assassination would precipitate World War I, was still very much alive, and you could buy a whole bag of love-hearts for a halfpenny.

I was two years old when World War One was declared, and I suppose, as I became more aware, I was conscious of the war in many ways. There was the rank, evil-smelling margarine, the chemical taste of 'honey-sugar', in a crude, brown, cardboard container, the skim-milk, the lack of protein, the ration books. Frequently mother made us all a basin of hot 'bread and milk' with sugar, and put us to bed. Mother and Father, Margery Wordingham and Arthur Jary, both came from the smaller coastal village of Stiffkey, about 20 miles east of Heacham. They were married in 1910, and the renowned Stiffkey Rector officiated at the wedding. I hear that he afterwards attended the reception, as did the whole village of two hundred souls, and he gave some amusing monologues as part of the entertainment.

By 1917, they had had five children in quick succession. It was time to call a halt; Mother was very ill after the birth of the fifth. There was Margery, the firstborn in 1911, then myself in 1912. With the arrival of Norman in 1914, my mother began to wonder where they were coming from and felt that she should know more. She ran around to a neighbour friend and asked her to explain why she was always getting pregnant. It seems odd nowadays that a girl brought up on a Stiffkey farm should have known nothing of the facts of life.

Mother's sister Daisy Wordingham knew even less, and to the end of her days - she remained a spinster - she was afraid to sit on a public lavatory seat for fear of 'catching a baby'. Victorian daughters were kept in blissful ignorance; it was part of their purity and virginity, and even living on a farm did not seem to enlighten them. Mother had seen the batch of eggs in a hen while preparing it for table, and she believed that she, too, had a batch of 'eggs' that would result in babies coming all her married life. It was a very sobering thought, because her own father, born in 1854, had been one of sixteen brothers and sisters, some of them twins. I do not know whether my mother was ever enlightened by her friendly neighbour, but two more children were born in 1915 and 1917, before Mother was able to piece together the mystery of pro-creation, and then only very vaguely.

My first really distinct recollection of a particular day must have been in 1916 when I was nearly four years old. I was going to stay with my mother's father Sam, Grandpa Wordingham, at Stiffkey, on the farm, for the first time. We were at Heacham station, junction for the Wells and Fakenham line. Mother was tying a label into the buttonhole of my lapel. It said 'Joan Jary, Passenger to Wells, care of the Guard'. I had a little 'portmanteau' full of clothes. She handed me to the guard and I was put in the little recessed seat in the guard's van. I swung my legs, and I could not touch the ground, I remember.

I was not in the least perturbed about the handing over. We knew Mr Pooley, the guard; he lived near us in the village. I knew I was going for a short stay to Mother's father at Stiffkey. It must have been discussed at length in my presence, at home, because I understood the guard would hand me over to other grown-ups at Wells, and there would be a ride by pony-trap to Stiffkey. I knew Grandpa Wordingham at Stiffkey farmed the Glebe Farm and lived with Aunt Polly. Polly, then in her forties, was his second wife, whom he had married at the turn of the century when she was in her twenties and my mother was about 15. She had not been much older than the little family she came to mother, and everyone called her 'Aunt' Polly - she was too young to be called Grandma. She had never had any children of her own, and when she saw we had a superabundance at Heacham, she very much wanted to adopt me, but mother would never part with one of her five, although times grew harder and harder between the wars.

A quick kiss, the guard blew his whistle, waved a green flag, and we were crawling away from Heacham. I seemed to be the only passenger, no doubt partly because it was wartime, but I

6

never did see more than half a dozen passengers on the Wells train. In the guard's van I had a muzzled dog for company and two large bundles of rhubarb. Heacham, Sedgeford, Docking, Stanhoe, Burnham, Holkham, Wells. As we stopped at each station the guard got out, passed the time of day with the stationmaster, and looked at his watch, on a chain in his waistcoat pocket. No wonder it took nearly an hour to get to Wells. The hill at Docking was always too steep for the engine and we could make no speed at all until we had left Docking behind us. At Stanhoe we deposited the rhubarb on the platform. At Burnham (change for Nelson's birthplace) we put out the dog with the muzzle. Not a soul got on or off the train. At last there was a long run round Wells and into the station, where stood the connecting train to Fakenham, waiting for the hypothetical passengers who just might materialize.

7

Mr Pooley was as good as his word. He took me by the hand and carried the portmanteau, and we walked the length of the Wells platform. I can still remember the smell of steamed rice that came from the Fakenham engine. At the station entrance I saw that there was indeed a black pony and trap, and therein sat Grandpa Wordingham and Aunt Polly. They tipped the guard, they lifted me high into the trap, put a great grey 'ghillie cloak' from Scotland around me, and made a fuss. A tickle of the whip, and the black pony, Tommy, began his four-and-a-half mile trot home to Stiffkey. The last thing I recall of that momentous day was that Tommy had to stop at the level crossing on the Stiffkey road to let my train go through back to Heacham. 'There goes your train back home!' I felt a momentary pang of homesickness, though at the time I could put no name to it.

The road between Wells and Stiffkey runs a little away from the salt marshes, and the hedges were then very high, and in the autumn smothered in red berries. They gave some protection from the winds that blow from the marsh in winter, and in the days of pony-traps protection was essential. At this part of the coast, if you look at a map, there is no land between Wells and the Arctic Circle. My father would say, 'You can just go on swimming out of Wells and come to the North Pole'. Indeed, some days, swimming in the North Sea, I could well believe it.

Just before Stiffkey there were glimpses of the sea, a blue line on the horizon beyond the salt-marsh, and then we came to Muckledyke, with a windmill and the dip down into the village. Cottages of whitewash and flint, very much as they are today, stood along the road, their back gardens running down to the river. Some had yards of flint cobbles.

At the Cross we turned right over a humped bridge, and up the hill to Hill House. Hill House, at the south end of the village, had a large, rambling garden surrounded by a high-sided chalk-pit. There were cowsheds, a pigsty, a grassy hummock which we called the 'pightle', a tub-house and dairy, and the house itself, white and flint again, a long double cottage built on the hill at three levels. There were even two caves up in the chalk to explore. This house and garden became my Garden of Eden for the whole of the time I was growing up, and I spent every summer (and what wonderful weather it was!) and sometimes other parts of the year in this delightful playground.

Hill House, Stiffkey 1916-18

If the food situation was desperate in 1916 at Heacham, and in many parts of England, mostly towns, there was certainly nothing to worry about in Stiffkey village. Perhaps that was one of the great advantages of being off the map. Compared with Heacham, we lived in unashamed luxury. We kept chickens, pigs, geese, cows, so we had plenty of fresh egg custards, roast chicken, geese, wild duck from the marsh, pheasants, which are almost tame in Norfolk, venison from nearby Holkham Hall, and an abundance of hares and rabbits. There was a garden full of red, white and black currants, strawberries, gooseberries, pears, plums, damsons, apples, and a fresh jug of cream every day to go with them. Grandpa Wordingham had about seven cows in milk, and next to the tub-house where we pumped up the water each day there was a little dairy.

Edna Engledow I loved. She must have been in her twenties then, a village girl employed partly to milk cows, make butter and supervise the dairy generally; partly she nannied me. I had long golden curls then, and she would sit me on the kitchen table and gently comb out the knots. She would wash me before meals, or take the little silver button-hook and do up the row of buttons on my ankle boots. We all wore boots, and there was a button-hook with a silver handle lying on each dressing-table upstairs.

Edna also played the piano in the sitting-room to me when she had a few moments to spare. She played the war songs; I helped with the singing - I had heard her sing them so often. There was a great, round world with clouds about it on one song-sheet cover. 'Let the great big world keep turning...' we sang. This was how I discovered that the world, although it appeared flat or undulating around me, was really a big ball, and we lived on the outside of it, with an envelope of clouds. I was not surprised, either, that it was

9

**Edna Engledow with Margery
aged 6 and the author aged 4**

always turning round, never still. Children will accept all these amazing things at an early age and not question them. I was having my first astronomy lesson. 'Good bye-ee, don't sigh-ee, Wipe the tear, baby dear, from your eyeee.' I thought that song was the best of all. I could give quite a spirited rendering of 'Bonsoir, Old Thing, Cheerio, Chin Chin, What ho! Toodle-oo! Good bye-ee!' There was a certain sadness about all these songs really. All the sons of the village were away at the war, all the daughters were left behind for four years, working in the cowsheds, the fields, up on the stack, and some went away to be Red Cross nurses. 'Keep the home fires burning' I thought was very sad, and I made myself miserable singing it over and over again.

Edna came at seven in the morning, milked the cows, pumped up water in the tub-house, and I usually awoke to the sound of her grinding coffee in a little machine in the dairy. Soon, while the coffee percolated, she would be starting the breakfast. While sausages, mushrooms, liver and eggs were cooking, she would bring up to us hot, soft water in jugs and knock at each bedroom door. The smell of rainwater and Cuticura soap and the aroma of coffee - what a lovely way to wake up every morning. We came down about eight.

Sam, my Grandpa, would never go off to the farm until the postman had been with the newspaper and letters. They were anxious days, how bad I did not realise at the time, since the war was all I had ever known and I had come to accept it as a part of the order of things. But Grandpa and Polly first looked for letters, then spread out the Eastern Daily Press on the table, turned to the long pages of casualties and studied them closely. Sons Sam, in his thirties, and Vincent, in his twenties, were on the Western Front, and they must reassure themselves each day that young Sam and Vincent, and other village boys, were still alive. The names were in alphabetical order and listed wounded, dead or missing.

I would go off to the dairy, to see Edna put the morning milk through the separator (we were very slightly mechanized). Milk ran one way, cream the other. There were also a number of large shallow pans where cream settled, and I helped to skim the cream off the top - thick, golden cream, wrinkling as I drew the skimmer over, and enjoyed every moment. In the afternoon, clean-scrubbed Edna (did she never rest?) put the cream in a hand-churn and we turned it. I loved to hear the 'clop, clop' as the butter formed. Then Edna would take some carved wooden butter-clappers, and I watched her, fascinated, as she banged, patted, turned, lifted and gradually produced a row of little half-pounds of butter, slightly salted, glistening with wet drops. She patted a pattern of little thistles on them. She also made dishes of little butter-balls for table use. There would be home-made loaves for tea, baked in a wall-oven in the kitchen, and big square-ended strawberries from the garden, dairy butter, and lashings of cream.

Before Edna went off duty at three in the afternoon, she would prepare the tea for Polly, especially if we were going to have 'fourses' up in the harvest field. Then she would pat buttermilk on my face and leave it to dry. The idea was, that if I wore my pink-print sunbonnet with its large frill, and patted on buttermilk several times a day, I could prevent freckles. Alas, I had bright golden hair, and there were so many freckles on me that you could hardly separate them - they were merging into one big round freckle! I was always sunburnt, and Aunt Polly and her sister Phoebe also wore sunbonnets like mine 'so as not to get sunstroke', so perhaps, after all, the summers really were hotter in those days.

On this particular morning that I remember(it was 1917), Grandpa opened the press before going to the fields and he and Polly began to scan the casualties, starting with W as usual. There it was at last, the worst had happened: Second Lieutenant V. R. Wordingham, missing, believed killed, at Ypres, Polly read. She gave a cry and fainted. Polly was the only person I ever knew who could drop down like that, just as they did in Victorian novels. Vincent was the youngest of the family of four children she had

11

taken on when she married Grandpa, and he was her favourite. I had never seen a faint until then, and I was mildly concerned. I knew where she kept the remedy.

'Joan, go you and git the smelling salts off the mantelpiece.' I ran into the sitting-room and fetched the little green bottle with the glass stopper. Aunt Polly was now on the sofa and there was a great loosening of stay-laces. Edna was called in too. The unstoppered bottle was waved about under Aunt Polly's nose and presently she revived and had a cry. I had, in the course of prying, tried those salts myself on one occasion. They were acrid, but interesting, and caused the nose and eyes to weep. Grandpa went quietly off to the farm, and I realise now how he must have felt the blow. He adored his children, and all children, and suffered silently. So young Vincent, jolly, good-natured, humorous, gifted, the one who had left home and gone to college and become a schoolmaster, died in his prime, and for what? He had married only a few months before.

'Joan, when you git home to Heacham,' they said, 'don't tell your mother about your Uncle Vincent. She's not fit to know yet.' Mother had just given birth to her fifth baby, a boy, and she had had a long and difficult time, and much chloroform. A few days later, when she was still rather ill, she thought her brother Vincent stood at the foot of her bed, and smiled. It was so vivid, she thought he was really there, and showed him the baby boy, and said 'I shall call him Vincent after you.' She was much too ill to go to the christening, but the boy was called Vincent as she wished.

Some days later, I came home from Stiffkey again, found her in bed, rushed up the stairs, and in my eagerness for her attention, cried: 'Mummy, Uncle Vincent is missing.' I was very important. My sister Margery, a year older, was furious with me. She came over, smacked my face, and said: 'You know we were not to tell her that!', and then Margery got into trouble for smacking me. But the secret was out. Mother lay there and cried weakly for a long time, and I felt so rotten.

Young Sam, my uncle, came home on leave from the front soon after this, and it may have been compassionate leave. Did they have any compassion in 1917? He was going to be posted to German East Africa. Lucky Sam - he survived the war!

I was at Stiffkey again. Mother was slow to recover, and the children were dispersed temporarily. I remember being snatched

12

from my bed very late one night, to be shown to uncle Sam, who had just arrived from Wells resplendent in his uniform and knapsack. He was exceedingly weary, and might just have walked from Wells. Impossible, I suppose, to convey to them just what it was like on the Western front.

A few nights later I was again snatched hastily from my bed. I was wrapped in a blanket by a very agitated Aunt Polly and in bright moonlight we all went up the garden path and into the chalk caves at the chalkpit end of the garden. One cave was new and short, but the one we used when Zeppelins came over was a very old cave that ran right under the Hall Hills, how far, where, and why, nobody quite knew. There were about twenty people in the

cave. We sat on some long forms which had once been school furniture, so we could rest our arms on the desks before us. A blackout curtain was at the mouth of the cave. We whispered fearfully. Overhead, Zeppelins hovered and droned and vibrated noisily.

On bright nights they came in low over the Norfolk coast, very near, and seemed to take a long time to pass, going so slowly. I was really frightened, expecting bombs to drop at any moment, and the chalk cave, precariously propped as it was, to bury us alive.

My father, Arthur Jary, was at Stiffkey that week, visiting his own family who lived in the village by the river. Father had some binoculars, was delighted with these Zeppelins, and was actually halfway up the slope of the pightle, watching them go back seawards, driven by two little fighter planes of the Royal Flying Corps. Presently he came running excitedly to the cave. 'You can come out, you can come out! They've brought one down in the sea!'

We streamed out of the cave, the relief was tremendous, and we ran up the slope, from where we could get a view across the village to the North Sea. My father handed the field-glasses to Polly, who looked, exclaimed 'It's all in flames in the water, I can see the men getting out!' and fell down in one of her faints. I was able to retrieve the glasses and have a good look at the burning Zeppelin, lying in flames across the water, and the men in the water, while they all helped Polly. Someone said: 'That's not for a child to see,' and took away the glasses and had a look himself.

I remember how utterly relieved I was at the sight of the downed Zeppelin. Now we could sleep in peace. The war was over, I felt, the Germans were dead. I thought: 'There will never be another Great War, I'm getting it all over while I'm young'. I really believed that phrase 'a war to end war', coined I think by H. G. Wells. We went back to bed with a cup of cocoa, and during the next weeks pieces of wrecked planes, Zeppelin, and bodies were washed up along the coast. It was said that Pat Colman of Norwich, of the Colman's Mustard family, had brought the Zeppelin down.

Alas, there were other Zeppelins, particularly one Christmas at Heacham when Aunt Daisy was staying with us. We had hung up our five stockings. We spent one night crouched under the living-room table, while that droning noise went on for a long time overhead. I knew Mother and Aunt were terrified. Father was outside on Special Constable duty. He came to tell us a bomb had fallen harmlessly in the lake in Heacham Park, and the next day it was dredged up and photographed. It was a great pear-shaped iron object, and photographs of it were on sale for many years in the village.

The next thing I remember about the war, was peace. My mother bought us each a flag from the village shop, and mine was a blue Australian one with stars on it. I ran round and round the block with it, and played with it for hours. It was the nearest thing to a toy that I had had for six years. We had, after all, beaten the Germans and there would be no more Zeppelins.

Vincent Wordingham, who was killed at Ypres

The Writing on the Wall

By 1920, we were all five at school, and I expect Mother heaved a sigh of relief. Even Betty and Vincent, four and three years old, went into the babies' class in the Infants' Department. We had a well-built 'Board School' at the top of the hill, a hundred yards from our house in High Street. It is still there and in good order. The school bells would ring as we finished breakfast, and then we all scuttled up the hill and into the school yard just in time.

There were three rooms: the babies' room for under fives, Class 2 for the fives plus, and Class 1 for the sixes plus. After that, we would transfer to the 'big school' until we were fourteen. Even in the babies' room we learned to read and count. We had a giant book hanging on the board at the front, and teacher would turn up the pages and touch with a pointer. 'In, pin, tin, sin,' we chanted in unison. 'I, in, is, it, if.' I was hypnotized, fascinated, I adored this game. We had all learned our letters first in a sand-tray, writing them correctly with our forefingers. I loved this too. There was, of course, no shortage of sand in Heacham. We had a whole beach of it to play with, but the sand routine at school was absolutely riveting. Teacher said it, and we wrote. Then she came to admire it. 'Make a b' - she showed us one on the board with chalk, and we had to begin just as she showed us. All the little forefingers began. Teacher came to see. 'Good, good, good. Now shake your trays. We'll make g.' We all shook the tray slightly, the sand was level again, and we made a new letter.

Everyone could read and knew the letters by the time they were five, and we were quiet, industrious, well-behaved for our tender years, except that brother Norman once decided to pour the sand from his tray on to the curls of the girl in front. We were horrified. Teacher marched him into Class 1 and told Miss Utting, who was the head teacher and rather feared. Miss Utting sat at a large high-up desk on a platform.

'I know where I shall put naughty little boys like you', and she pushed him into the dark kneehole under her desk, and went on writing in her register. There was a long, subdued silence, until Norman could bear it no longer and sank his teeth into the calves of her legs. 'Ow!' cried Miss Utting. 'You bad boy, you have bitten my leg!' We had a hard job not to show our delight and satisfaction. Sister Margery was in Class 1, and had to take Norman home by the hand and tell Mother. I am sorry to report that there was a great deal of mirth at home too. Miss Utting was none too popular.

Well, by the time I was five, I could read and write well, and graduated to slates and slate-pencils. The slate-pencils may have been a hangover from 1870, or may have been used to save pencils and paper in wartime.

It was not all work and no play. We had bricks, a rocking-horse, dolls, a rag-bag for fraying and a maypole. We learned a number of singing games and maypole dances, we had fairy tales and rhymes, and I read an enormous number of fairy-tale books, which was just as well, because the reading primers were old, tatty and of the 'fat cat is full of cod' variety. On the whole, we were all very happy at infant school, and I do not know of anyone there who could not read and write. But how we would have enjoyed constructional toys, crayons, paints, Wendy houses, and the physical education apparatus schools have today. Because of the war, we still had no toys, and there were none yet in the shops. It was as a fluent reader and a cursive-writer that I next turned up at Stiffkey and put my new skills to good use.

In the parlour at Stiffkey there were two windows. One looked out on the street, the other at the garden and the Hall Hills. There was a sofa with embroidered satin cushions and a whatnot full of knick-knacks in one corner. There were many lamps trimmed ready to light, and two hung from brass brackets on the fireplace. There were some elegant shells displayed and an ostrich egg in a silver mount, which Uncle Sam had brought back from German East Africa after the war.

But on a little round table lay the family Bible. It was huge. It also contained the Apocrypha, and was copiously illustrated. Inside the cover, in faded brown ink, were the names, dates of birth and deaths of many of the Wordingham forebears, lovingly recorded by fond parents, grandparents, great-grandparents. I began to read all

17

the 'best' bits of this Bible. It was a revelation, especially when seen with the accompanying pictures. Noah's ark, just setting sail, with wretched, wicked people begging to be taken aboard, on the point of drowning. Noah was adamant and noble. Moses was taking off his shoes in front of a flaming, unidentifiable shrub. Jonah knelt praying in the belly of a whale. Best of all, there was the look of horror on the faces of Belshazzar and his guests, as fingers spelt out trouble on his palace wall. 'Mene, mene, tekel, upharsin' appeared against the candlestick upon the plaster of the wall. The king could actually see the half-a-hand doing the writing. Consternation on every face.

I looked around for a thick black crayon. I selected a large area of cream-distempered wall with no impedimenta. Now, what to write? I searched through the commandments, which we had just been learning at Sunday school. I decided on 'THOU SHALT NOT COMMIT ADULTERY'. I didn't quite know what it was that adults got up to, and this commandment was never properly explained in school, but it had a good, rounded sound. I started by one window, and I soon had it writ large right across the wall, in letters six inches high, just like the writing at Belshazzar's feast. I stood back, and saw that it was good, just as Aunt Polly appeared at the door. 'Jinky-Bee', (why did she call me that?) 'come and wash hands, it's time for dinner.' She took a step down into the parlour, saw the writing on the wall, and turned white. We had her on the sofa, and I had to fetch the little green bottle with the glass stopper. She recovered quickly, and it was action stations. She rushed in to Grandpa and told him all. He was not angry; I thought he was laughing a little as he said something about 'out of the mouths of babes and sucklings...'. But Polly was not easily consoled. Nobody in the village must know! She drew the curtains of the window that looked on the street, and sealed the door of the parlour. As there was no key, she had to seal it with tape, as if the room was to be fumigated. There is no doubt about it, I reflected, writing on the wall is a great success, has repercussions.

Aunt Daisy says that I had my 'beatyem' smacked and was sent to bed. I remember nothing of that. We had a good dinner. After dinner they sent for a discreet relative who was a builder and decorator, and he brought all his paraphernalia on a donkey and creamed the room from top to bottom, restoring the status quo.

'Flu 1919

'Every year has a number, and that's what you call it', said my elder sister Margery. We were standing in the front garden at Heacham. It was some time in late spring, because in the shingle of the front garden pale blue-flowered squills were pushing up between the stones. At the turn of the century, this land on which our house was built had been a donkey meadow, and squills grew wild.

'This year has a name,' pursued Margery. 'It's called Nineteennineteen.' I digested this for a while, but everything Margery said was so. She knew.

'Who said so?'

'We wrote it at school.'

A few days later we were again picking squills and I recalled the name of the year. 'It must be Twenty-twenty now,' I said.

'No, the years last longer than that.'

Why do these little incidents make such an impression in childhood? A few unimportant but vivid mornings get imprinted for a lifetime. Perhaps it was our first morning out after we had all had the Spanish 'flu, and so was cause for celebration. When peace descended on us in November 1918, the shops were not immediately full of goodies, clothes, or comforts. Only gradually were there improvements, and there never was any money, anyway.

My father had the influenza first. He was always susceptible to it, and probably brought it home from his shop. He had to get up and nurse us all, after a week. He was getting better as we all went down with it. Norman, Margery and I had it next, and we thought it the worst cold we had ever had. We had to stay in bed quietly all day, with noses bleeding. We had nightmares, but Mother was now getting too ill to help us. She had it last, with the two youngest, Betty and Vincent, in bed ill beside her, so that she could watch them.

What a misery, to have influenza so badly, with two toddlers in the bed, three children convalescent, and a depressed husband rushing home at midday to feed the family! Those weeks we had influenza after the war were even sadder than anything we experienced during the whole war. Every house was affected, whole families were ill at once, and there was a quiet over the entire village. Many houses lost someone in the family, the curtains were drawn here and there down the High Street. The doctor's family were all ill. He sent a message round to us all to 'stay in bed, have plenty of hot milk and oranges, and get up gradually'. He would come again when he was able, but there was nothing he could do to help further.

Mother was still in bed with her two toddlers. They were all ill. Margery and I were dressed, but very subdued, watching at the bedroom window, to see father come down the street, home to make dinner. None of the women who usually helped could do so now. The village was at a standstill.

'Here comes Daddy!...He's got a bag of oranges...He's taking off his hat,' we said.

'Where is he?' asked Mother.

'By Pull's cottage.'

'Oh dear!'

When Father appeared, with hat still in hand, he said: 'The blinds have just been drawn at Pull's. It must be Stanley.' He went downstairs and took from the oven two large rice puddings. Before he went to the shop each morning, he would mix up rice, milk, sugar and several eggs into two large dishes, and put them in a slow oven. At lunch-time, there they were, having cooked gently all the morning. They were delicious: creamy and hot, just right for us in our convalescent state. We all ate, and had a large orange each. At night we had a big bowl of bread and milk. So we all survived.

The depression stayed for some time. I remember my utter despair, as I stood by the sink one day, and sister Margery's nose bled and bled. There were, of course, no tissues in those days. Mother tore up a sheet upstairs, and got back into bed. I ran to Margery and stood by the sink with her, handing pieces of rag to her as she needed them, convinced she was dying.

Children are resilient and, come spring, we were soon making our rabbit-hutches again, gathering sow-thistle, dandelions, poppies and hogweed from the hedges, collecting pondweed for the tadpoles, picking our cowslips, feeding silkworms. We really didn't need any toys, but we did have whips, tops and hoops. We lived near Rodney, the blacksmith, and father got him to make us some iron hoops. We had iron hooks to run them too. Father made us whips and tops. Indeed, he made whips and tops for most of the village. Children would appear in his shop and ask: 'Please Mr Jary, will you put a new toe in my top?' He was never too busy.

He was a bootmaker, as was his father, and generations before them. They had come over with the Huguenots and the tools of their trade, and settled in Norfolk. There are still many Huguenot families in East Anglia. My father remembered that his great-grandfather still spoke French and gave lessons in French in Stiffkey. Old Andrew Jary, who died in 1724, has the oldest of the Jary tombstones in Stiffkey churchyard, and I believe his name may really have been André. The boots and shoes were all hand-made and bespoke in those days. A pair would last for years and years. They made button-boots out of soft leather for ladies, little boots for children, riding-boots for all the local gentry, and farm boots for labourers. My father also made special orthopaedic boots for the King's Lynn Hospital. It was a dying trade, there was no future in it in the twentieth century. When he retired in the 1950s he must have been one of the last of the real old-fashioned bootmakers. I remember when we were all very small, he bought a soft, white doeskin and made us five little pairs of boots out of it. Mother was so proud of us, in our little white boots!

But more and more the shop became a shoe repairer's and retailer's and people ceased to buy bench-made footwear.

21

Stiffkey Caves

The garden at Stiffkey really occupied a large disused chalkpit. Long ago, the chalk and flints had been quarried out of the side of the Hall Hills. At one side, a flint wall separated us from the Hall Farm. We had a row of beehives there. At the back were chalk cliffs, with the Hall Hills beyond. They were not too steep to climb, and filberts and walnut trees grew on the slopes. The garden was nicely sheltered from all winds, ideal. I have picked a bunch of wild violets in the chalkpit on New Year's Day, and wild yellow wallflowers at Easter.

At the back of the little outdoor privy grew a fig tree, and the fruit ripened regularly. On the end wall of the house grew white grapes, and Polly made a lot of jelly. On the side of the house grew the most luscious Victoria plums I have ever had the good fortune to taste. The drive leading round to the cowsheds was lined by a gooseberry hedge said to be nearly a hundred years old. There were red gooseberries, green dessert gooseberries, cookers, and 'golden drops'. There were loganberries, and black, red and white currants. Roses, laburnums, lilac, peonies crowded everywhere.

While Grandpa Wordingham, in his straw hat and black veil, was smoking out the bees, I would go and explore the chalkpit caves. 'Keep you away from here,' he would say as the bees objected. 'Git you out.' I shot off to the caves, although I was afraid once I was inside. I was just afraid enough to enjoy the sensation.

Outside the cave was a broken-down old sleigh. I would sit up in it and play the Snow Queen and fancy myself. I was told that only a few years ago the winters had been so bad that they had regularly driven the sleigh instead of the trap, and had put bells round the horses' collars. 'The horses loved it. They would shake their necks again and again to hear the bells ring.'

Eventually I would pluck up some courage and enter the cave a few feet at a time. You had to go slowly, I discovered, to give your eyes time to get accustomed to the dim light. After a few yards, the cave forked left, and went only ten yards further. Here were stored the old desks we had used when we sheltered from those Zeppelins - so long ago that seemed already. But the right fork was a larger and older part of the cave and ran darkly right under the Hall Hills. I went very gingerly along, waiting from time to time to let my eyes accustom themselves to the gloom. Why did I never bring a candle? We had plenty, and torches in the house. I don't think I really wanted to go too far in alone. The village noises seemed so far away when I was in the cave.

The chalk smelled wet and stale. My pace would slacken. I knew that nobody knew I was in the cave, that if the roof fell (and it was very crumbly) no one would find me there ever again, until I was a skeleton, just like the story of *The Mistletoe Bough*. With that, I would rush back out of the cave, being careful not to stamp my feet too much as I went. The fresh air and sun were such a relief.

What were the caves at Stiffkey? Were they old flint mines? Is there another 'Grimes' Graves' under the Hall Hills? All those flints for the cottages and walls around the coast must have come from somewhere, and Breckland is a long way. Grandpa, as a road contractor to Norfolk County Council, still took cartloads of chalk from one part of the drive, and would pile up flints as he came upon a layer. He sold flints too. Some were very large and irregular.

Were they smugglers' caves? The marshes were still being used for rum-running in the nineteenth century, and the caves may have been used for storage before Hill House was built and the garden turned. My father remembers that his Grandfather Jary (who lived to be nearly a hundred) once had a very vivid dream that he saw two kegs of rum (or was it brandy?) lying on the marshes between Stiffkey and Morston. He was so excited about it at breakfast, he could describe the exact bushes where the kegs lay, and would have the boys go 'down Bangey' - the greenway to the marsh - and walk east towards Morston, and just look for him, as he was unable to walk so far. The boys went, to humour him, actually found two kegs washed up the creek by the tide, and brought them home. In his youth, he must have known the 'rum paths'. Even when my mother was a girl (she was born in 1884), young girls and boys were urged *never* to go along the marshes at night, especially in the moonlight, or 'the great shuck dog' would get them. The monstrous shuck dog (a shuck was a ghost) was the same one that crops up in ancient Fenland lore, but I think the idea of resurrecting it on Stiffkey marshes was so that people would stay away from there late in the evening and at night, and would see no more than was good for them.

So the caves may have held kegs of brandy and rum, but perhaps were very old even before that. Occasionally, the rum-runners were drowned, and washed up in the creeks, for the marshes are very treacherous when the tide comes in, and the rickety wooden bridges over the creeks soon get covered with water, or lost in the mist. To keep warm, it is said, the men would bore a hole in the cask, insert a straw, and suck the rum or brandy as they walked. It is not surprising, then, that some fell into the creeks or stepped on the wrong bridge. Mother remembers that drowned smugglers were brought up from the shore on a farm gate, and laid out in the Glebe Farm barns near the church, until the coroner pronounced it was 'misadventure'.

Some people said the caves were part of a complex of underground caves linked with Walsingham, a place of pilgrimage a few miles away with even more ancient connections. If there were as many caves connected with Walsingham as people say, most of Norfolk would have subsided long ago! Some maintain they were connected with the underground passages at Fiddler's Hill, two miles away.

One morning we received a mysterious letter from Spain (or was it Portugal?) when the postman came at nine. Grandpa was absolutely astounded. It was addressed correctly to him, in a copperplate handwriting, and he fingered it for a long time before breaking the seal. This must have been about 1925. Eventually he opened it, and found the letter was written in the same neat hand on thin squared paper, rather like airmail graph-paper. 'It's a furriner,' he said. 'Here, you read it, Daize.' Aunt Daisy was home for the summer, and she read it to us.

Two sailors, in Spain, wished to assure Mr Wordingham that they knew of some treasure buried in the caves in his chalkpit. They had seen it buried some years ago, and they knew exactly where to dig it up. If he would send them five pounds, they could come by cargo boat to Wells, and on to Stiffkey. If he could provide the shovels, then they were proposing to dig up the hoard, and would share it with him fifty-fifty, since it lay on his property.

'Who are they, Daize? When did they put it there? How long ago and how old are they now? How did they know that I have the house now?' He mulled it over for a long time.

'Father, we don't want foreigners coming and digging in those caves while we are asleep!' Aunt was very nervous. I was delighted.

'Oh, send the money! Do let them come, Grandpa!'

At last Grandpa agreed to tell the police, on Aunt Daisy's insistence. Now we seldom saw a policeman in those days. Nothing ever happened in Stiffkey. The Constable lived two miles away at Binham. If you wanted him, you made it known at one of the inns, and at last the policeman would hear that someone at Stiffkey wished to see him and one afternoon he would cycle over. It was quite a social occasion. We loved having visitors. The policeman came in, had a whisky and soda, and went round the garden and was given honey, damsons, pickled walnuts, whatever was going. It was a courtesy. Everyone shared garden produce.

At last we came casually to the business. 'I have heard that you wanted to see me about something, Sam.' The letter was produced; they went and had a look at the caves. The policeman read it again. 'If I were you, Sam, I should just tear it up and take no notice on 't.' They stood, and tore up the letter and threw it away, and I was horrified. 'There's a lot of fellows unemployed these days, and come home from the wars, and never got a job yet, and they'll do anything to get five pound out of you. Don't you send it!' Perhaps he was right, perhaps not. Aunt could not forget the incident. On a moonlit night she would say 'Do you think there are men that know the other end of our caves, and they are digging in there?' The caves would have to be blocked up before she had any peace of mind.

A few weeks later my father came on one of his visits to Grandfather Jary in the house by the river, and was going to take me home to Heacham when he returned. About this time, his grandfather's donkey died, having long outlived its master. I came upon my father and his brother, my uncle Lewis, bearing the donkey on a five-barred gate and walking up the garden of Hill House towards the caves. 'Come and see this, Joan,' he said. 'It's a dead donkey. You won't ever see another all your life.'

'Why not?' I asked. 'Don't donkeys die?'

'Hardly ever,' he said. 'This one is over ninety.'

'Where are you taking it?'

'Your Grandpa says we can bury it in the cave, under the Hall Hills, as we can't bury it near the river.'

So the dead donkey was put in the cave, a little way under the hills, and they took pickaxes, and brought down the roof, and blocked the passage under the hills for ever. The whole cave is in a dangerous state today. The Spaniards never materialized.

Nine Hundred Flowers

The South Beach at Heacham was a two-mile strip of sea-turf, perhaps fifty yards wide, between the shingle beach of the Wash, on one side, and the Heacham River on the other. At high tide it was much narrower. Before a dam was built at the river mouth, and the water diverted to a culvert, this was a tidal estuary which we called 'the harbour'. The marsh by the river was then full of shrubby sea-blite, locally abundant bushes (two-starred for rarity in the botanical books), and there were sea pearlworts, sea lavender, sea asters and purslane. On the short sea-turf and dunes, which became a long peninsula to 'the point' at high tide, we could walk along through clumps of sea-holly (enjoyed by blue butterflies), past areas of brave sea campions, yellow stonecrop and sea bindweed. There were hollows filled with yellow horned poppies, and the turf underneath was springy with haresfoot trefoil. Pink restharrow grew spikes in this dry salty habitat, and there were minute varieties of hawkweed and sea cranesbill.

The longer grass was full of larks' nests, and the song was incessant. On the shingle beach at the point, you could pick up amber, jet, and mermaids' purses among the shells, and come upon whole families of arctic tern chicks in their striped camouflage, or clusters of sea birds' eggs barely distinguishable from the pebbles. You felt that this had been so for centuries, ever since the retreat of the ice age.

The whole area should have been protected. Alas, the dam was built in the 1930s across the mouth of the river, and changed the ecology of the marsh by the 'harbour'. It is almost a freshwater pasture now, and cows graze there. Herons still dip for eels, and get them too. Teasels and ragwort grow everywhere where once were sea lavender, asters and purslane. The water is brackish. It attracts many swans, but how much was destroyed to produce just one more grass meadow for cows?

Ringstead Downs, sheltering an ancient trackway in its hollow, is about one and a half miles from Heacham, a little way inland from Hunstanton. Here is another timeless spot where the flora must have remained unchanged for centuries. The same close turf full of rock-rose in June, and selfheal, ground-ivy, thyme and violets. In the chalkpit by the track grow cowslips, primroses, speedwells, milkwort and lady's bedstraw. I was nine when I first found a blue milkwort, and it was such a revelation that I had almost a spiritual experience, and all the way home I composed a poem about it!

In the woods at the Ringstead village end of the downs are the finest wild arum (parson-in-the-pulpit) you could wish to see, very early at Easter, among the celandines. Cuckoos sing. It has been so for a thousand years.

On Holkham beach I once found a broomrape growing parasitic from the root of sea-holly, and pointed it out to my father. 'Do you know, Joan, there are over a thousand species of wild flowers in England, and nine hundred grow in Norfolk,' he said.

Certainly nine hundred grew around Stiffkey, and I knew where to find them, and when, at any time I visited. There was blue chicory in the field beside Phoebe's cottage, on the Home Hills. By the path under the flint wall of the rectory (alas, they have widened the road since) were great clumps of purple clary, spicy and aromatic to grab and crush and smell. I knew where, in the Home Meadow, there was a patch of white violets, and year after year it never disappointed me at Easter-tide. Down the Arnold (every field had its own lovely name) in the swamp by the stream, grew winter heliotrope, smelling deliciously nutty like almonds. Cowslips were in the Glebe, and later we picked mushrooms in the same places. The river was then full of trout, and lined with brooklime and forget-me-nots. In the light of East Anglia, the blue of forget-me-nots really is unforgettable. Viper's bugloss was abundant. The corn was full of poppies and field campion.

After harvest, I loved the miniature gardens that grew up between the stubbles. I would lie face down in the stubble very close to the ground and stare at the miniature versions of flowers I knew. The fields were so dry and sandy 'down Bangey' that dwarf forget-me-nots were only one inch high, and there were tiny hawkweeds just one inch and a half, perfect in every detail. There was also a scattering of scarlet pimpernels, wide open, proclaiming the heatwave.

As I investigated, Mr Bensusan, the well-known essayist, would sit on the greenway, on his shooting-stick, a typewriter in front of him, typing away hour after hour. We never disturbed one other. He was doing his thing and I was doing mine, and each disregarded the other. I wish now that I had chatted with him.

If you walked 'down Bangey', the path led presently to the marsh. Long grass full of harebells gave way quickly to wormwood (deliciously bitter, and good to smell when you were ravenously hungry) and then purslane, thrift, asters, pearlwort, sea lavender, all the way along the coast for miles.

I must mention here a particular little green plant which grows in the mud near the creeks: glasswort, 'a curious, succulent, salt-loving plant, with no obvious beauty,' to quote the botanical description. But to us it was known as marsh samphire. We bought it by the pint at the door, and cooked it, and had pickled samphire for tea in August and September. With home-made bread and dairy butter it is as delicate as asparagus and much cheaper.

By the river at Stiffkey, 1925

Feeding Swallows

Grandpa Wordingham was getting increasingly lame in one hip. 'Go you, Joan, up to the Yards, and take a stick, and bring home the old sow and her pigs, and shut her up in the sty up in the garden. Do you think you can bring her?'

'Will the little pigs come? Will they get lost?' I was rather unsure.

'Jest you look after the old 'un. The piglets'll foller her.'

So off I went to the Yards, by the Stiffkey Church knoll, and opened up, and took a stick that was lying nearby, and drove out Susan, the blonde curly sow. She was huge, and she 'umph-umphed' all the way, but once on the road she knew just where she was going, and a troop of little piglets followed her. Fortunately there was not a lot of traffic in those days, for this was the coast road to Cromer. Down Church Street we went, and Susan turned left at the Cross. She knew the way, and led her pigs over the bridge, then, just as I thought we were home and dry, she stopped. The sight of the river was too tempting for her and she decided to go down where the horses go, and give the family a drink. Down she went into the river, and down went her fourteen piglets after her. They had a good drink, and perhaps if you were feeding fourteen piglets you would have a thirst that size. Not content, she began to wallow in the shallows, and all the piglets followed suit. They would never have done this for Grandpa, he would have given them the big voice. But they seemed to know it was only me. Eventually, with the aid of Mr Engledow, who saw the pigs were fouling the water, we got them back on the road, and in their own good time we reached Hill House. I put them in the sty. They knew the way perfectly well. I ran in to tell Grandpa how I had fared at the river. 'Oh yes,' he chortled a bit into his beard, 'she allus dew that.'

I would go up to the sty, at the top of the garden, with a big stick, and lean over and scratch Susan's back, and she would grunt appreciatively. So it was one day, when we were en rapport like this, that I observed several swallows flying in and out of the open doors of the cowshed, next to the pigsty. In the rafters of the shed, when I investigated by standing up on the manger, there was a row of swallows' nests, all clay and feathers, and several little baby swallows, mostly well fledged, were crowding at their windows and demanding food vociferously. I watched them feeding for a time, and the parents were really so busy that they did not mind me, and carried on non-stop with their task.

Now, the cowshed doors, which stood wide open (we no longer had dairy cows), had a large round hole near the bottom to allow cats to enter to feed their kittens or catch mice when the doors were shut. The barn doors up at the Yards also had cat and kitten holes. But what I now noticed was that there were some smaller holes near the top of the door, to allow swallows to fly in and feed their broods in early morning and late evenings when the doors would normally be closed.

I was intrigued. Swallows and storks have always been popular; but nobody would show such kind consideration to sparrows or starlings. Is it because the swallows are harbingers of spring, or because they so obviously eat their own weight in flies and midges every day? For how many centuries have farmers carved bird-holes in the tops of barn doors to accommodate parent swallows?

I had read somewhere that swooping swallows can do sixty miles an hour, and I thought, 'How clever, at sixty miles an hour, to speed through that tiny hole!' I decided to shut the doors and wait to see what the swallows would do when they came back with their beaks full of flies. So the doors were shut, and I waited. I did not have to wait long. Some poor swallow, who was certain that the doors had been wide open a moment ago, came whizzing back, tried for the hole at the last moment, banged her beak on the door, broke her neck and fell dead at my feet. I was aghast, desolate. I opened the doors again, and propped them open lest any moment another swallow should fall dead.

I picked up the bird, warm and bleeding. The neck was broken, I knew. I felt vile just then, a murderer. If I had killed a friend I could not have felt worse about it. I thought the world would never be the same again now that I had killed that mother. But that was not all of the horror. I wanted to hide the bird so that the other birds would not see what I had done. Dispose of the corpse and the evidence. Gently I dropped the mother swallow into a pile of straw in the pigsty. To my utter disgust, Susan sprang forward, snouted about in the straw until she found the bird, and then crunched it up, still warm, feathers, beak and all. Now it was truly dead and I was even more distraught. Never, never again would I scratch Susan's back for her. That was all finished.

By this time there was a great clamour, in the cowshed, of young motherless swallows demanding flies. I went in, climbed on the manger, and watched with an aching heart to see which nests were being catered for and which babies had no mother. I soon identified the nest. There were four swallows, fully fledged, quite a good size, but wanting hundreds of flies urgently. There was nothing for it, I should have to spend the rest of my holiday filling matchboxes with flies from morning to evening, and ramming them down those four throats, and serve me jolly well right. Just then, Aunt Daisy called from the kitchen door. 'Jinky, come and get ready for dinner.' I had to go, but I would be back.

During dinner I had a heavy heart at the prospect of the next week, and the burden of this guilty secret. I must eat well, smile and talk naturally, and try not to let them see something had happened. I chatted, keeping one eye on the cowsheds which were just visible from the dining-room window.

As soon as dinner was over (and they made me dry the crockery when Ruby washed up) I waited until Grandpa was having his forty winks, which was an after-dinner nap of about one hour. I was free! I rushed out and straight up the garden, but after several minutes I had only two flies in my matchbox. This was not going to be as easy as I had thought. Anyway, I would take in the flies when I had four, and give the birds one each to be going on with. Later, with four flies and a beating heart, I climbed up on the manger under the motherless nest. I was about to push a squashed fly into a gaping beak when to my amazement a swallow came and fed the babies for me. In a few seconds, another swallow arrived. Swallows were feeding flies to their own, and then visiting my nest and giving my orphans a few. They had adopted my birds! I was so delighted and relieved, I crept away after I had seen enough. I stood experiencing pure joy. God was in Heaven, had seen it all, and moved in His Mysterious Way! At that moment I was prepared to believe that he even leaned out of the clouds and caught the falling sparrows, as they told us in Church. Never again did I ride on the old sow's back or scratch her with a stick. I never forgave Susan.

The Wordinghams

I wish I could have met my great-grandmother Wordingham, for when I piece together her story, from what Grandpa kept telling me, I think she must have been a remarkable woman. Her life shows the hard time that women, and men too, had in Victoria's England.

Elizabeth, along with her husband, migrated to the North Country and settled at Bacup in Lancashire. There was a mass migration from Norfolk to Lancashire with the industrial revolution and the development of factories and machines. This must have been in the late 1840s when Victoria was still young and my great-grandparents were newly married. But Elizabeth was the real worker, her husband, like many men of his time, always drunk after a day at the mills. She missed her home and the Norfolk skies, and she also produced a baby every year with unfailing regularity - and sometimes in duplicate. She decided she was going to get back home.

She was one of those tall, broad, raw-boned descendants of the Vikings, with frizzy golden hair, blue eyes, and as strong as an ox. Norfolk is full of Viking types. She was as energetic and deter-mined as her husband was indolent. She meant to get back to Norfolk with all her children, so that they would never have to go to work in the cotton mills. She wondered how she could possibly save enough money to get away from Bacup, since her husband drank everything.

One day she decided that, as he wouldn't dig the garden and grow some food, she would do it herself. She took a spade and, to her surprise, found a seam of good coal, just below the surface, on the land behind their house. Her problem was solved. She would dig that coal, bag it herself, and she even humped it on her back round to all the neighbours. Everybody used coal then, and Elizabeth prospered. In a few years she was able to transport the entire family back to Stiffkey, where she bought Vine Cottage. I don't know whether great-grandfather reformed, or died exhausted after fathering sixteen children.

Most of Elizabeth's children survived to be octogenarians, and at one time I had great-aunts and uncles in all the villages from Stiffkey to Sheringham, with glamorous names like Clarissa, Laurissa, Florissa, Marianne and Georgianna. Some were twins. They were all alike to me, well corseted, with elegant black gowns down to their boots, and their necks elegantly supported in cream lace, boned to just below the chin. They had faded auburn frizzy fringes, blue eyes, and large frames. Reading George Eliot's *The Mill on the Floss*, I later recognised my great-aunts in the character of Mrs Pullet. It has often been said in criticism that Mrs Pullet was just an exaggeration and a caricature. Quite wrong! There really were people like her - all my great-aunts, and perhaps many more in East Anglia and elsewhere, and they had about them a great deal to be recommended.

My own grandfather, Sam Wordingham, was well down the list, about fifteenth in the family. Isabella, who died in 1950, was the baby. The eldest of this great brood was 'Captain' Fred Wordingham of The Ship Inn at Brancaster, who could be seen for years propping up the window sill outside the tavern. He wore a sea-captain's hat and a dark blue fisherman's jersey, but had never been to sea in his life. This was my grandfather's favourite brother and, to the end, even when they were both past seventy, they called each other 'boy'. 'Harness you the black pony, I'm a goin' to Brancaster to see the boy Fred.' And when we arrived: 'Why, here come the boy Sam!'

There was no family allowance and no social security, nor even pensions. One wonders how those people survived; but they certainly did, and all lived to a ripe old age. Great-grandmother sat her large family all round the room, on benches, as there was no table big enough, and they had bowls of bread and milk for supper. There was no free education in the villages until 1870, and then not until the school was built, but she sent them all to Dame School, and it cost her fourpence a week for each one. There was a Dame School at Stiffkey, kept by one Old Bet Jary, but that is all I can find out about it, or her, and she does not appear to have been a relative of ours.

My grandfather had to leave the Dame School in 1865 when he was nine, then go for a few years to a boys' school in Warham, a village near Wells-next-the-Sea. He had to walk there and back every day. By this time he had had much experience of helping with horses, and knew that that was what he wanted to do. When one of the Queen's doctors, who was visiting the Stiffkey Rectory, asked him if he would like to come up to Scotland and be a groom at the Queen's stables in Balmoral, Sam was thrilled. It was a wonderful chance for a young boy in those times, and Sam accepted the offer. He was fourteen.

So his mother packed all his clothes and possessions in a big black wooden sea-chest, and it must have been a sad parting for her. She would not see him again until he was a grown man. In those days (this was in 1868) you went by sea to get to Scotland, taking a boat from Wells. Many boys had to leave the village to find work, and many went into the Navy from Norfolk. Girls had nothing to look forward to but to go into service in one of the big houses which abounded in Norfolk, until they got married, if they ever did.

Grandpa had never been to sea before, and as the small ship hugged the coast and kept putting into port to shelter from gales, he was extremely sick all the way. The journey took several days, and he vowed that if he ever got a foot safely on shore again he would 'save all his bawbees' and go home by the newfangled railway. He never went to sea again. Several years later, when he had 'seft enough bawbees', he came back by rail and lived with his brother Fred at The Anchor Inn in Morston, the next village to Stiffkey. While in Morston he worked the oyster beds and ran oysters by pony to the Norwich trains, for London hotels, each day. He also ran a carrier business to Norwich, collecting parcels and delivering goods to houses in villages. He later moved with his first wife, Elizabeth, to the house in Stiffkey.

I never tired of hearing those stories about his adventures with the Queen. He was at Balmoral for about ten years, and his duties were to look after the horses and train the Queen's black pacing-mares. They all had to keep exactly in step to pull the carriages.

He knew John Brown well, and 'niver liked the man'. He thought him pompous and very conceited, and unpleasant when he spoke to the servants. On one occasion, when young Sam had not long been there, and it was damp and drizzling, he took a short cut across the courtyard, his head well down, and found himself face to face with the Queen and John Brown on a narrow path which he was not really allowed to use. Sam was confused. 'Take yer cap off, boy,' shouted John Brown at him, 'don't yer know you are in the presence of Her Majesty?' Sam whipped his cap off at once, even more confused. 'No, put it on again quickly, Sam,' said the Queen quite kindly. 'You'll get your hair wet in this weather.'

Every Saturday evening there was a dance in the Hall at Balmoral, to which the servants were also invited. The pipers were there, and there were reels and sword-dances. Sam enjoyed these occasions, soon learned the Scottish reels, and had danced with all the princesses. He loved to say: 'Princess Alice, Princess May? Yes, I've often had a dance with them, many a Saturday night.'

Sometimes Sam accompanied the Queen on her walks around the village of Crathie. John Brown was invariably in attendance. Sam was actually present on the occasion of the 'soup story' which is often thought to be apocryphal. It was quite true, and Sam would tell it like this.

'As we were walking up the street the old ladies would be sitting at their cottage doors, with the doors open. A delicious smell came from one of the open doors and the Queen walked across and asked John Brown to enquire for her how the soup was made, so that she could send the recipe to her daughter. The old lady told the Queen: 'Well, ma'am, there's onions in tult, carrots in tult, turnips in tult, and barley in tult.' And the Queen said to her: "Yes, my good woman, but what is tult?"'

We had to hear the same old stories over and over again, for Grandpa enjoyed his memories of Balmoral. By now in his middle age, he was a lookalike of Andrew Carnegie, and once or twice when he returned to Scotland to visit his old haunts, he was mobbed wherever he went, because people were so sure he was the great industrialist and philanthropist who had gone to America to make his fortune. When he settled at last in Stiffkey, he used his Scottish nest-egg to rent the Glebe Farm. The farm consisted of a few fields around the Church and Rectory and another area 'down Bangey' towards the marshes.

The Church

Mother was ambitious for us all. She wanted us to have an education, and an interesting career, and get away from the village, and not have to stay around home as she had been obliged to do. She began to buy Arthur Mee's *Children's Encyclopaedia* for us, as it came out in weekly parts. We read these instalments as fast as they appeared. It was a good idea at the time. Suitable books for children were few and far between. Our house was not without books: *The Life of Tennyson, Palgrave's Golden Treasury* and a lot of *The Sixpenny Poets* which my father had collected in his youth as they were published. He could recite all these poems too: Hood, Byron, Shelley, Cowper, Wordsworth, Gray, Coleridge. He loved sea stories, so we had Rider Haggard and Captain Marryat. Great-grandmother Elizabeth Wordingham had been housekeeper to Captain Marryat, who lived nearby in Cockthorpe, before she married and went to Bacup, and his books were very popular in Norfolk.

It must have been in the *Children's Encyclopaedia* that I found a long poem, in which every verse ended:
'Some call it Evolution
And others call it God.'
I loved this. Father had been a great reader of Darwin, and had explained to us about the evolution of species and the survival of the fittest, as he understood it. Mastodons, dinosaurs, brontosaurs, we believed in them rather than Adam and Eve. Every Sunday we were duly sent off to Sunday school, then on to church, where we sang in the choir for several years. I noted that Father and Mother never went to church although they had been brought up to it, and to a rather strict régime. When Mother was a child, everyone curtsied to the vicar when they passed him in the village. She was

**Margery Wordingham,
Mother, before her marriage**

rather indignant, however, about that, and never would do it. Still, they were confirmed and took communion.

When I was fourteen or so, Miss Katie collected about ten of the likely girls and began to prepare us for confirmation in Heacham church. I suffered this, not very gladly, and wondered at the time why girls were being confirmed but boys were not. Perhaps the boys successfully dug in their heels. Two years earlier I might have accepted it without question, but now I began to query everything. The words of some of the hymns, in particular, were very peculiar. When we stood up to recite the Creed, I began leaving out the things I was not quite sure about, and soon there was very little of the Creed I could honestly stand up and declare I believed any more. Phrases like 'blood of the Lamb' and 'sinful lusts of the flesh' sounded especially meaningless to me and fell on stony ground. As the vicar (stone deaf, very elderly, and I could barely distinguish his words) droned on about how sinful we were, and that we had been 'born in sin', I somehow felt that none of this applied to me. I couldn't believe any baby was a sinner automatically.

I was still praying by the bedside each night, as we had all been taught. Whenever we were at Stiffkey, I slept with Aunt Daisy, and we prayed by the bed before getting in. More and more my mind wandered, and I sometimes found myself making up the thirteen times table by mistake!

Aunt Daisy always suffered dreadfully from flatulence, and as we prayed, she would invariably stop in the middle of a sentence, strain, and produce a prodigious fart, and then carry on devoutly as if nothing had happened. I would stop at six times thirteen, and turn to her and say: 'How on earth can you do that, Aunt? If you're talking to God, how can you make Him wait while you do that?' Aunt could always see the funny side, and would start to giggle. 'Yes, I really shouldn't do that, Joan, should I? He might have been listening!' I thought: 'If He's not listening, what are we doing anyway?'

So it was with very mixed feelings that I began to prepare for confirmation, hoping that I should be sorted out in time. But I never believed that I had been born in sin; the word 'adultery' was still a mystery, along with the facts of life.

We began to learn by heart:

'Question: What is your name?

Answer: N or M.'

A bit silly, I thought, and the rest of the catechism did not impress me either. It seemed to me, as a young teenager, to have been written long ago, by some men, for people in the early centuries. I could not see how it could be relevant to me. 'What a pity', said Miss Katie one day, when I had actually questioned one of her definitions in order to be able to understand it better. 'What a pity your father - such a nice, kind gentleman - is an atheist!' I was astounded, as I had never regarded him as an atheist. The word had quite a dreadful ring as she pronounced it. She made it sound as bad as 'Bolshevist' and that was the worst possible word in those days.

My father was one of nature's born gentlemen. With a family of five it is surprising, but he had never had to spank a single one of us, and I never heard him raise his voice unduly to any of us. We would do anything immediately that he said, and we loved to help him. He was one of a family of six boys and a girl, and his mother must have been a wonderful woman. I never met her.

Most of the village owed him money at the shop. It was like that in the gay twenties, there was so little money circulating. Food was very cheap, but still we could afford so little. Everyone had a young family to feed, and father did not like to send in the bills. On Saturday evenings people would come into his shop for a chat on their way home from The Greyhound, and offer him a sixpence towards the shoe-bill. Father would pull out a well-thumbed ledger and cross sixpence off the bill. Alas, the bills grew as fast as, or even faster than they were paid off.

Father was so considerate that I have seen him peeling a ripe William pear in the garden, and dropping the parings down wet side up so that the butterflies could drink the juice on a hot day. 'Go carefully,' he would say; a red admiral would be sitting right

40

on the pear in his hand. Two or three more were drinking from the peels at his feet. 'Mind how you go! They like to have a sip of juice on a hot day. Don't tread on the butterflies.' The most he ever saw drinking at a time, he told me, was eleven, and at eighty-two he was still entranced with watching butterflies slake their thirst.

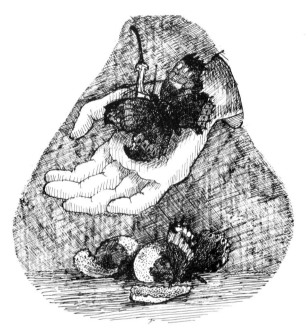

Well, I was confirmed eventually, and took my first communion. I was going to Stiffkey the following day to spend a week with Aunt Daisy, so I decided that I would take my next communion at Stiffkey with her. Aunt had just become the headmistress of Stiffkey school, which was a church school, and one of her duties was to play the organ for morning church. She would have done so anyway, because she was a practising Christian to the end.

But that Sunday morning I went with Grandpa 'up the Yards', to the meadow by the church to gather the eggs. He never worked on a Sunday, nor allowed anyone in the house to do more than was strictly necessary, but he did like to remove the eggs from the hens, and check on the animals. I would be home again in time to change for church and get my white gloves and prayer-book. We had Pat with us, the wire-haired fox terrier, and it was not long

41

before Pat caught his usual rat in the cowsheds. He always brought it straight to his master's feet, proud of his catch. So I took the basket of eggs, and Grandpa carried the bloodied rat by the tail, and we set off home along Church Street.

The first bell would soon be ringing for church, but there would be plenty of time, because the Rector was usually half an hour late. As we went along, we met the churchwarden coming up the road, and passed the time of day with him. In a village as small as Stiffkey, only two hundred souls, we would never pass without at least the ritual two-stroke exchange.

'Mornin', Jimma. What's it goin' ter dew?'

'Mornin' Sam.' Jimma noticed the rat swinging by the tail. 'Wha's that you got there? What are you a goin' to do with that there?'

'Oh, the dawg just got it, and brought it to me. I niver throw it away while he's a lookin'. That can't do the dawg good. I'll pop that over the rectory wall as I go past.'

'Oh, don't yew dew that,' said Jimma. 'Give yew that ter me, that'll dew fer my ferrets fer dinner.' He took the rat and stuffed it into one of his jacket pockets. 'I'm orf to ring the bells, but Rector's not here yit.'

Suddenly he pulled the rat out again, pretty quickly. 'Oh, my Gawd! I've put that there feller right on top of the communion bread!' He transferred the bleeding rat to his other jacket pocket, fumbled and extricated a hunk of unappetizing bread which he carefully dusted, then returned to the ratty pocket.

'Well, do you hev ter supply the bread then?' asked Grandpa.

'Mostly, to be on the safe side,' said Jimma. 'When Rector come at the last minute, he rush straight in an' I hev the bread ready for him. He nearly allus fergit the bread.'

'Go you on then, and ring that bell,' said Grandpa, and we continued down the road, he musing and with a twinkle in his eye. 'Doan't you say nothin' to your Aunt about that,' he said, and just at that moment we met Aunt at the crossroads, coming round to church, best costume, and hat, and white gloves and prayer book.

'Are you coming, Jinkie? There's time to get changed and catch me up.

'I don't think I'll come after all,' I said.

'You must come to communion. It's your first Sunday after confirmation, and this is communion day.'

'I know. I'll just leave it this week.'

Grandpa thought he had better tell her after all. 'Daize,' he said. 'If I were you, I'd not stop to communion today. You tell him you can't stop, and come you straight home after the service.'

'Why, father? Is anyone coming to dinner?' She became suspicious. 'I'm playing the organ. Besides, I'm sometimes the only one at communion, and I couldn't very well walk out if it was all prepared.' Now he felt he had better put it to her more plainly, and he told her about the bread and the rat in the pocket. She raised one hand to her breast, then gulped. 'Should I go home for some more bread?'

'No, there's no time.'

'Father, once it has been blessed, the bread is purified, it turns into the body of Christ, and it can't harm anyone.'

'Well, you can eat that if you like,' said Grandpa.

'*Honi soit...*' said Aunt, and went to church.

I never did take communion again. Aunt Daisy suffered no ill effects from her devotion to duty.

Collecting water at Stiffkey Bridge, 1926

Home Entertainment

Our house at Heacham was called 'East Lea'. The front door faced east, the back door faced north, and the cold winds blew straight in in the winter. If both doors were open at the same time, there was a great slamming of doors and windows all over the house. For a large part of the year, the house was a cluster of ice-boxes. I do not know of anyone who had central heating in all those years, and it was well into the twenties before electricity came to the village. We just had a large wood and coal fire and took a candle and went upstairs to bed. It must have been a tremendous relief to Mother when we had electricity at last, and an electric iron.

Most evenings after tea, especially on Saturdays, father Arthur would go back to the shop until nearly ten o'clock; but on Sunday evenings, after tea, we had good fun with him. On Sunday afternoons we would go for a walk, perhaps three or four miles. It might be to Hunstanton cliffs, or Ringstead downs, or the south beach, or Sedgeford, and when we came home we were quite ready to do justice to those special teas. Mother went to bed for a couple of hours, then got up in time to set a specially nice tea-table. There were eggs and cress, lots of celery, which was delicious because we grew our own, large plates of Mother's buns, and a cake, or oranges, and sometimes jellies. We brewed many pots of tea. After tea, since that was the warm room of the house, it was a social occasion. Father would entertain us, and we just sat there egging him on and on.

'Say Johnnie Jones' - this was Norman's favourite. It must have been one of those Victorian poems learned for the Sunday school anniversary, and it went like this:

'Oh, Johnnie Jones, why do you do it?
Those who throw stones surely will rue it!
Someone is watching, armed by the law.

44

Soon from his pocket, truncheon will draw.
Off he will march you, dreadful to think,
To a dark prison, light through a chink,
Bread without butter, water to drink,
Bolt, bar and shackle, spike and high wall! -
Ah, that is better, let the stone fall.'

We were all petrified. There was a tremendous crescendo, arms gesticulating, the voice gradually rising to 'Spike and high wall!' - then a pause and a quiet 'Ah, that is better, let the stone fall.' Norman's eyes would be popping out of his head at the idea of a little boy in prison, his jaw wide open. In the silence after, we would all take in an audible breath, and Daddy would laugh. Then, all together: 'Do it again, Daddy, do it again.'

Sometimes we asked for 'the rivers'. Father had been only to the little village school at Stiffkey, in the early days of free education, when you sat and learned a great deal by heart, and teachers were paid by results. Children were empty vessels to be filled up quickly before 'the inspectors' came round. They learned their geography by the 'capes and bays' method, and this was the rhyme for learning the rivers of the British Isles.

'Thames Ouse Trent Humber Tees Wear Tyne and Tweed
To the Germanic Ocean or the North Sea proceed.
The Tamar the Avon the Exe and the Wey,
To the Channel of England much rubbish convey.
The Severn it rises in Plynlimmon Hills,
And passing through Shropshire receives other rills.
Through Worcester and Gloucester it then doth proceed,
Where rivers do add, and wide it doth spreed,
And when it advance twenty miles further on,
The Channel of Bristol declare it is gone.
The Eden, the Ribble, the Mersey and Dee,
Discharge themselves into the Irish Sea.
The rivers of Ireland I'll name if I can,
The Shannon, the Liffey, the Boyne and the Bann.
And then into Scotland I must take a ride,
To visit the Dee, the Tay and the Clyde.'

Years afterwards, when my parents had their silver wedding celebration, we all paid for them to go to Cornwall for a holiday, by car. It was the first time they had been away together since they were married. When they returned, Father was full of excitement and I asked him how he had got on in the south west. He was bursting with something. 'Joan,' he said. 'Do you know, there is a river down there called the Camel - and one called the Parrett!'

Sometimes we asked him to recite Wordsworth's 'Lucy Gray'. We liked being made a little sad.

'Oft I had heard of Lucy Gray,
And, when I crossed the wild,
I chanced to see at break of day
The solitary child.'

We followed this in silence. It was very sad, about the little girl who got lost in the snow, and whose footsteps went to the river bridge, and then –

'Into the middle of the plank,
And further were there none.'

Another poem that tore at our hearts was Tennyson's 'The May Queen'. The little girl was dying.

'I thought to pass away before, and yet alive I am;
And in the fields around I hear the bleating of the lamb.'

She took a very long time to die, and no doubt went straight to heaven.

Wordsworth's 'We are seven' was a favourite. 'The Wreck of the Hesperus' by Longfellow was another. Mother liked Tennyson best. She had a very low, straight-backed chair, on which she nursed all her babies. She told us it had once belonged to Tennyson's mother, who had nursed the poet there. I think this might have been true, because it had come from Captain Marryat's house in Cockthorpe village, and the Tennysons used to stay there. None of our possessions at Heacham or Stiffkey was ever new. Grandpa always went off to the auctions at 'the big houses' when he wanted to replace any furniture, and this was widespread practice. Most people set up house like that, for years. So, our table in the living room was a solid mahogany drop-leaf, a hundred or so years old even then, and there were Queen Anne bureaux, bow-fronted drawers with brass handles, old sea-chests, davenports, brass-knobbed beds that would now be worth a fortune, and marble-topped wash-stands. At Stiffkey, Grandpa slept in a gorgeous four-poster bed of carved mahogany, from the Hall. It had a canopy, and scarlet curtains could be drawn around. The pillars at the foot were beautifully twisted. You could lie in it, close the curtains, and be Queen Elizabeth. Beside this bed was a

little sixteenth-century wooden crib, a cradle in which he rocked
his four babies. It swung from a frame, and was still in good
working order.

So Father entertained us on Sunday evenings, and many other
evenings before he went back to the shop. He would give rides to
the two youngest, on his foot, and sing:
'Bumpety bumpety bumpety bump,
As if I were riding a charger,
Bumpety bumpety bumpety bump,
Just like an Indian Rajah.
And all the girls declare,
He must be a gay old stager.
Hey, hey, clear the way,
Here comes the Galloping Ma-jor!'
When the fun was over, we went to bed. I do not remember ever
having a fuss about bedtime. We were happy, and tired, and ready
for bed, and we just lit the candles and went up.
Sometimes, if it was a bright moonlit evening, we would go out
first to see the Milky Way. The Norfolk skies, often wonderful by

day, can be a revelation by night, and the displays unforgettable. Father would show us the Plough, the Pole Star, Orion, Castor and Pollux, Mars, Venus. We have watched many a display of Northern Lights, shimmering green curtains around and above us. The day sky, too, was not without its phenomena. Once or twice we saw 'mock suns' across the Wash, and sometimes an inverted mirage of Hunstanton Cliffs was visible above the horizon over the opposite side of the Wash. On one occasion we saw several mock suns together, with multicoloured haloes around them, and overhead a pattern of intersecting rainbows. 'It is a parhelion', said Father.

One night there was an unusually beautiful display of Northern lights, and the Milky Way was particularly brilliant. Father had just been reading all Sir James Jeans' popular astronomy books, and now he looked up for a long time before he spoke: 'You know, Joan, we are all just pismires,' (the Norfolk word for ants). 'Mankind in space, we are just a lot of pismires.'

Mother and Father in 1928

48

Changes 1925-1927

Margery was thirteen, due to leave the village school. I was nearly twelve. We were both at the top of our class, and mother had not the slightest idea what would happen to us next. There was nothing for a girl to do in the village but go into service, or work in the Hunstanton or King's Lynn shops. Boys might perhaps work on the land, or at building, or go into the army in despair. Most young people, and many older ones, were now out of work. Unemployment was even worse in towns, because townspeople could not keep hens, grow vegetables, and survive by barter.

We had an enormous quantity of onions. Father collected his own seeds by tying a paper bag over a large onion-flower. He planted two ounces of tiny onion seeds one year, and they all came up, two hundredweight of huge golden onions. They lay for a few weeks on groundsheets around the yard, and dried beautifully. One day he hung a row of thick strings, each about a yard long, on our wire linen line. He tied a single onion firmly at the bottom of each string. Then he showed us how to select only the best hard-dry onions, and twist them on to the string. Off he went to the shop, and we carried on with the stringing. We loved to please him. When he came home for dinner, we would have a great number of strings of onions, hanging on nails around the yard, on the sheds, everywhere. Twopence a string, we would receive. It was a great treat, for we never had any regular pocket money.

Of this great onion surplus, he would give many strings away, anonymously; just walk around and hang onions on a nail by the door of friends, neighbours, any old folk who lived nearby and might need them for the winter. Sometimes they, too, would have a surplus, and when we looked out in the early morning to take the milk in from the doorstep, we often found mysterious bundles of rhubarb, a couple of cauliflowers, a red cabbage, a bag of gooseberries, never quite sure who had put them there. I have no doubt this little exchange is still going on on most of the back doorsteps of Norfolk.

Well, we survived, but Mother began to realise that time was running out, and she must 'do something about the children' before we left school. She dearly wanted us to be teachers, like Aunt Daisy. There was only one way to make a little extra money in those days to send Margery to the Lynn High School for Girls: she would take in some summer visitors, and earn the few pounds a term required to send her to Lynn. Lynn was sixteen miles away. There would be train fares, packed lunches, school uniforms for five years. So, during the summer holidays while some of the girls were at Stiffkey, and the boys away at scouts' camp, Mother, helped by Margery, began to take in summer visitors. More and more people were coming down on the main line from London to Heacham and Hunstanton for seaside holidays. Hardly anyone went abroad, and seasides in Britain were always full for a few weeks. The season was short, but Mother was so pleased with her first year's savings - forty pounds.

Margery started at the High School, and Grandpa Wordingham considered the idea. For a man born in 1854, with so little education, he was wonderful. He came over to Heacham one day, and said that we must all be served alike, that if Margery went to King's Lynn we should all go. Nowadays, he said, a good education was absolutely essential to get a decent job in life. He had purchased £2000 worth of War Loans and now he decided they should be transferred into my mother's name and all the interest spent on the children's education. What a fortune in those days! Being a very fair man, he then gave his son Sam and his other daughter Daisy a similar amount of money each so that he had treated all his children alike! He was not rich, but he could just afford to do that, and in those days, perhaps, it was riches compared with the poverty of many large families in villages. It was the luckiest thing that happened to us, and it changed our lives.

So we left the elementary school and began to attend, the girls at the King's Lynn High School, the boys at the King Edward VII Grammar School, also in Lynn. The boys had red blazers and caps, and we had Lincoln green blazers, navy gym tunics, thick black stockings, thick navy bloomers, black shoes, and straw hats with a green school ribbon. There were tennis racquets, hockey sticks and pads to buy, geometry sets, boxes of paints, satchels and pencil boxes. I had never had anything like this before, and the school uniform was the smartest thing I had had for years. I was delighted with it all. We also had season tickets on the train to Lynn, lasting a whole term at a time, and we could travel backwards and forwards as we liked. It was affluence.

I suppose we had not realised before that, just how deprived we really were. Very few children in the village made it to the High School. We were almost the only ones in a village of two thousand. Scholarships were few and far between. What terrible waste and neglect there was in those days of depression!

At first we were so thrilled that we travelled up to Lynn sometimes on Saturday mornings just for the ride. My seven years at the High School were very hard in some ways, though. Mother had to be a very good manager to make the interest on grandfather's money last five children for seven years! She still took summer visitors to help feed and clothe us, and worked herself to a standstill at times.

We had to get up in the winter mornings at seven o'clock, in the dark, by candlelight, and wash in cold water. Mother or Father had a breakfast waiting for us downstairs, and we had to pack five lots of sandwiches and bananas. The packed lunch had to last us until six in the evening, when the train brought us back. We could not possibly have afforded the hot lunches which some of the town girls paid for, at half a crown a week. We rushed out of the house when we heard the Wells train coming round the back of the village. It just gave us time to catch the 7.56 from Hunstanton. If we missed it, we would have to wait hours for another train. I don't think we ever missed that train. It was a half-hour ride to Lynn, and there were special coaches at the end of the train, for schoolboys and schoolgirls. These were taken off at Lynn before the train went on to Liverpool Street. By the time we reached Lynn I was already ravenously hungry, and I remained so all day. I grew thinner and thinner. It was a long, thrilling day, and there were gymnastics and eurhythmics too. I could have eaten four lunches!

When the school doctor visited, I was pronounced too thin, very short-sighted (I had not known), and had sixteen teeth in trouble. It was recommended that I should have a drink of hot milk at school every day, and this would cost half a crown a month. The milk was lukewarm, had a lot of skin, but was comforting. There were biscuits for sale at break which looked delicious. I could have eaten them all. At four for twopence, I had to think how I could get some, since we had no pocket money, and I came up with a solution.

We took the weekly *Lynn News* on Tuesdays. The paper had a children's corner, and there were competitions. I found that, if I wrote a poem or a story, I could depend on getting a five-shilling prize. Oh, riches! It lasted about five weeks, then I would try again. I won the poems or stories; Margery won the drawings and paintings. Sometimes Betty would get a prize. We would say: 'Whose turn is it this week for a prize?' 'No, you had it last week!' We were so proud when, occasionally, our pictures were published, and when the 'wicked Uncle' from the paper came over one Wednesday afternoon to see the Jary family that kept getting all his prizes. 'Wicked Uncle' was Philip Schwabe, who much later, in 1942, married Betty and became our brother-in-law.

At Stiffkey, in 1925, Aunt Polly was very ill. She had had a cancer operation, much too late. She had a relapse. She had sent for me, wanting to see me before she died, and I think I must have known, although it was never spoken in words. I can never forget those few days at Hill House as Aunt Polly lay in bed in great pain. I sat downstairs at the little davenport and tried to read, with my ears well blocked up. I was re-reading, for about the tenth time, my favourite book at the time, *Manco the Peruvian Chief*, to keep my mind from the pain upstairs. Although under sedation, Polly moaned and gasped and cried out, and I could hear everything below decks quite easily. I was in anguish. She was only fifty-four, not much older than my mother, and she had been a second mother to me. She had done nothing to deserve this dreadful pain. It was the first time I had felt helpless in the presence of pain and death. Daisy was home, with Grandpa. We all suffered. I prayed again. I made a bargain with God - well, Noah, Abraham, didn't they make bargains? I said, if Aunt Polly got well, I would go to church and be good for ever and ever. He would not regret it if He spared Polly.

The next evening I was to go home on the bus to Heacham, and I went into the bedroom because Aunt Polly wished to say goodbye to me. We were very casual, but we both knew it was the end. I kissed her, and she made me show her the new school

52

uniform I was wearing for the journey. Her last words were,. 'Joan, be a good girl, keep this uniform clean and always fold it up on the chair before you go to bed at night.' We parted.

A few days later, I was in bed at Heacham. Mother came up-stairs with a telegram in her hand. 'Joan, Aunt Polly has died,' she said gently. Then she stood looking out of the window for a long, long time. So that was the way it was. God was not going to spare Polly. So there was to be no bargain, and, what was worse, I had a rotten influenza.

It was February 1925. The immediate result of Polly's demise was that Grandpa had nobody to look after him, and men never looked after themselves in those days. He had Vera Engledow, who came at

The author, aged 12

seven every morning and cleaned the cutlery, sharpened the knives, polished all the shoes and went home to breakfast, for five shillings a week. He had Ruby Jordan, who came (now that Edna had married) to make breakfast, clean the house, wash, iron, bake, get the dinner ready, wash up, and go home at three-thirty. She had ten shillings a week. But he needed a housekeeper to live in. Yes, you've guessed. Aunt Daisy was the spinster of the family, and was required to give up her position as headmistress of Wymondham Infants' School (and a very beloved one she was) and come home to housekeep for her father. She was in her mid-forties.

Such a sacrifice would be almost unheard-of today. But Sam was a Victorian father, loving, kind, dutiful, self-righteous, as honest as the day, a religious man although he hadn't attended church for years. It was Daisy's duty, he felt, and in return he would give her a good home and food, and what more could a daughter want? He honestly thought a daughter wanted no more, and would do her duty by him. Daisy had a good cry, but she adored her father, and had this great sense of duty too. So she gave up her headship, and her circle of friends at Wymondham, and home she came, sacrificing her professional prospects in the

53

process. That was how it was for so many maiden aunts in those days, and there were so many because a whole generation of men had been wiped out on the Western front at the Somme and Ypres.

Shortly afterwards, when there was a vacancy at the Stiffkey

school, she was persuaded to apply, and became head teacher there for a few years; but it was never the same for her again, and her final pension was minimal. It was a church school, and the Stiffkey Rector popped in occasionally to give the children a lesson and take prayers. He also required her to play the organ at church on Sunday mornings, and this was not without its excitements. I would blow the organ with bellows at the side, when I was staying with Aunt; she would play and sing. A few seconds before the responses, or

Aunt Daisy after retirement

before the prayer ended, one had to anticipate. Aunt would raise her eyebrows as much as to say 'start', and I would begin 'clump, clump' on the bellows, so that there was enough wind power for us all to sing 'Amen'. Sometimes there were only Aunt and myself at the organ, and about half a dozen in the congregation. On some occasions the Rector was ten minutes late, and the congregation had gone home. On other occasions, Aunt would say to me: 'We'll give him ten minutes more, then we'll go for a walk to the marshes'. I would immediately hope he would not turn up, so that we could have that lovely walk 'down Bangey' to the marshes.

'Bangey', I found later from an old map, was really 'Bengate', dated from Norman times and had got its pronunciation from the Norman French of the day. There were other signs of Norman occupation in Stiffkey as well. Demesne Lane, now known as Damson Lane, led to the old Hall, the one demolished when Sir Nicholas Bacon, Keeper of the Great Seal to Elizabeth I, bought the land on which his son Nathaniel built a new one in 1576. The 'New Hall' is now called 'Stiffkey Old Hall'.

But I have digressed. I was telling you about 'down Bangey' and this old Norman greenway to Stiffkey marsh. For centuries it was an access route to the Glebe meadows and cornfields, but it must have been used for years before, by fisherfolk, cockle-gatherers and smugglers. Mother said that from time to time a drowned sailor was brought up Bengate on a five-barred gate and 'laid out' in Grandfather's barn. He would say to her: 'Margery, don't go up to the barnyard today, they've laid a sailor in there'. Eventually, the corpse would be given a pauper's funeral and buried in an unmarked grave at the end of the churchyard.

So, to Bengate we went some Sunday mornings, arms linked, while Aunt Daisy told me the tale of *The Mill on the Floss,* bit by delicious bit. It was usually the summer holidays, with larks singing high over the fields, and purple sea lavender stretching out as far as the tideline, a blue band on the horizon. Sea wormwood and harebells were at the shore edge, with clumps of sea campion and thrift in the sea turf. A little higher up the bank there were rabbits, nibbling the close turf and scuttling into Coney Woods as we passed by. On the wet marsh, covered only a few days a month by tides, as the creeks filled, grew sea-spurrey, more thrift, sea-lavender, milkwort, sea asters, plantain, pearlworts, and, in the mud beyond the creeks - samphire. They always survived the high tides, the cold, the winds, and came up in abundance every year.

Sometimes we went cockling, but it was much easier to buy cockles (Stewkey blues) fresh at the door, and samphire by the pint or quart, and cook them ourselves. The samphire was baked slowly all night, at the bottom of the wall oven, in vinegar, water and spices. It was kept in stone jars in the dairy and we often had it for tea with bread and butter, or sometimes cockles.

We often saw the cockle-gatherers as they returned over the footbridges from the marsh, their skirts tied up with string, mud up to their knees, and carrying large baskets of cockles on their backs. They would chatter all the way, their sing-song Norfolk voices sounding across the marsh. If we passed a group of them making their way from bridge to bridge, Aunt would ask: 'Will we have time for a walk?' They were very knowledgeable about the tides and knew exactly when the bridges would be covered. 'You're all right, Daisy,' they would shout, 'but turn yew back in half an hour'. We knew they were reliable. After half an hour we got off the marsh.

You can still buy those cockles in pints. I doubt very much whether they will ever be decimalized.

The Rector of Stiffkey 1925-1931

On Monday mornings, as we waited on the platform at Heacham for our school train, the connecting train from Wells would arrive first, and out would step the Rector of Stiffkey, and look for us. He knew we would be there and he liked to travel down to Lynn in the carriage reserved for the girls, to while away the first part of his journey back to London. We would all pull out books and look over our homework. As the train stopped at Snettisham, Dersingham, and the Royal station, Wolferton, more and more schoolfriends got in.

We all knew the Rector. He discussed the poets with us and recited speeches from Shakespeare. He spoke beautifully, and should really have been on the stage or in Hollywood. He was also a great raconteur. We were soon abandoning our homework to hear his stories. He always had some jokes to tell, perhaps slightly risqué by the village standards of those days, but in no way was he ever vulgar, improper or suggestive. We laughed; he enjoyed his half-hour. At Lynn he moved to the London part of the train after waving us 'goodbye till next week'. He could easily have gained the reputation of pestering, as indeed he did later. In retrospect, I believe that if he had travelled in the boys' carriage instead of the girls', he would have been highly suspect.

On Saturday nights the Rector sometimes missed his return connection to Wells. There were very few trains to Wells, and he often had to spend the night at Heacham, and travel on by taxi to Stiffkey the following morning, arriving at the church just in time to take the Sunday service. He had been, for some years, a curate at Southwark Cathedral, and had been doing what he called 'rescue work' in slum districts of London, helping prostitutes especially. As there was so little to do in Stiffkey during the week, he spent more and more time away in London, and we all under-

56

stood that it was this 'rescue work' that took him there. I have certainly seen two or three young girls at a time, in their twenties and thirties perhaps, walking around the village. They were more smartly dressed than the villagers, and clearly having a holiday. The idea was to give them a few weeks' respite and country air with Mrs Davidson at the rectory, and, when they were well and truly rescued, to find them suitable employment, perhaps service in a good home somewhere, so that they were not obliged to go on the streets or starve. So, we knew they were around the village from time to time, and why they were being helped.

So, then, at the weekend, the Rector would occasionally find himself stranded at Heacham station for the night. Sometimes he sat upright in a chair in the waiting room and slept, which he found very easy to do. But at midnight the station master sometimes came to lock up and would turn him out. When this happened he would have to walk down to the village (about a mile) for a bed.

One night, after I had been asleep for an hour or so, I was woken by some unusual bumping noises above the bedroom. I held my breath; the bumping continued, as if a man was climbing over our tiled roof. Eventually I woke my sister Betty, who shared the room, and we both listened, terrified. Should we wake our parents? When, presently, a shower of shingle hit the bedroom window, we knew someone was there, and went to fetch Father and Mother. 'Oh, that'll be the Rector', they said, and went downstairs. And so it was. He had just been turned out of the station; he hated to bother us so late, but could he have a chair for the night? We were so relieved, Betty and I, and both went back to sleep. But Mother was too hospitable to leave it at that. She made a quick supper and, while he ate it, she came upstairs. Sister Margery was whisked out of her own little room and had to come and sleep with us. How we hated being three-in-a-bed! 'Come on, it's only for one night, go off to sleep.' Then Mother pulled off the sheets, put on new ones and made up the bed for the Rector in Margery's room. When at last he came up to bed there, I could hear him on the landing whispering: 'May I just peep in at the girls?'

'No, they're asleep - you'll see them in the morning.' But he insisted, opening the door, to our horror. We hated being seen three-in-a-bed. We kept our eyes firmly shut, feigning sleep.

'They're fast asleep' - Mother knew we weren't – 'I'll just leave
them these sweeties.' And he deposited two or three toffees on our
pillow.

The next morning, all up early to a nice breakfast, because
there was all the time in the world on Sundays. The Rector sat on
and on after the meal, and we talked and talked. We heard all
about how he had once been a padre in Egypt in the Great War.
We saw the picture of himself sitting on a camel by the Pyramids
to prove it. Time went by, and Betty said tactlessly: 'When I was at
Stiffkey last week you said there was going to be an early
communion.'

'Did I?' - and he looked at the clock in consternation. It was nearly eleven.

'If you don't go quickly there won't even be time for morning service,' said Mother, and rushed off to get Playford's taxi.

The Rector gathered up his belongings. 'And who's coming to Stiffkey for a ride?' He knew two of us would like to come in the car, visit Hill House for an hour and then return in the car to Heacham. Margery and I decided go; Grandpa and Aunt would love to see us. Off we went, at great speed, along the coast road to Stiffkey, and the Rector would be about half-an-hour late. Aunt Daisy, the organist, normally sat about half-an-hour waiting for him. After that, the few in the congregation would go, and soon afterwards so would she, for a walk down to her beloved marshes.

Along the way, the Rector took a few puffs at his half-cigar then put it away again. That cigar was like the widow's cruse of oil, never quite finished. Just outside Stiffkey, we stopped and he got down in the back of the car and donned his clerical garb so that when we arrived at the church knoll he could jump out and dash straight into the church. 'Take the girls to Hill House to see their grandfather,' the Rector would say. 'Mr Wordingham will give you the pound. Tell him I'll be along later.'

On this occasion, however, just as Mr Playford was about to drive us off, the Rector came rushing back out of the church. 'Stop, stop!', he called to us. 'Please do come in and have the service! I'm too late, they've all gone, but if you come in, I shall be able to write to the Bishop and report that I took a service with the remnants of the congregation.'

My heart sank as the taxi disappeared up to Hill House, but my sister and I were obliged to go into church first and be the 'remnants'. So we had the complete service, sermon and all. I pumped the organ, the Rector played it as he sang the service, and Margery sat in a pew and gave the responses loud and clear. There followed a very good impromptu sermon on the blessing of having good parents, and a secure home, and a splendid example of kindness and generosity from our mother, and so forth. We did not even squirm. Then I had to rush back to the organ to pump it up so that a few seconds later there was enough pressure for the Rector to play the 'sevenfold amen' and bless us. There was no collection, no passing round of the plate that day. We were as penniless as he was. He was a bankrupt, and Grandpa was paying all the Glebe Farm rent to the Official Receiver.

When we got back to Hill House, there sat Playford enjoying his elevenses, and Aunt, who had returned from the marsh, was delighted to see us. When Playford was ready to go at last, we collected from the garden a basket of windfall apples, cabbages, and a bunch of flowers for Mother, and a bowl of dripping from

the dairy and a brace of rabbits. There was always an exchange of gifts whenever there were family visits. What you had plenty of, you shared. Grandpa would pay the taxi, and home we went again.

In the afternoons, the Rector would come along to Hill House to pay his respects. He had a chat every week with Grandpa, and thanked Aunt for playing the organ. There was a great deal of gentle chiding, because Grandpa would never go to church, although he was a very god-fearing man. He would defend himself to the Rector. He was disturbed at the Rector's way of life and didn't believe in borrowing money. 'Do right, and fear no man,' Grandpa would quote.

Quick as a flash, 'Don't write, and fear no woman, Sam,' the Rector would call, as he scuttled away again. He was full of wit and quick repartee, a very cultured man. There was not enough challenge for him in the village routine. On Monday mornings he was away and up to London again by train; I think he had a season ticket.

In 1930 and 1931, fate caught up with him, and some of the girls he had helped to 'save' were used to bring about his downfall. Accused of immorality, he was to be tried by the Consistory Courts, and would conduct his own defence - there was no legal aid for the poor in those days. I think this was the only time my parents ever bought the evening papers, as did everyone in the county. It was trial by newspapers; the reports were so funny and the Rector's replies in court so witty, it was sometimes a delight to read, and he certainly scored his points. But alas, he was made such a laughing stock all over the country that from day one of the trial in 1932 there was no hope of an acquittal.

With all the details of his private life exposed, it must have been a great pain for his wife and large family of teenage boys and girls. Even before the event, crowds had begun to invade Stiffkey church at weekends, trampling over the graves and craning to get a better view. The Rector preached some splendid sermons; I have never heard their equal. He enjoyed the stimulus of a full congregation. Aunt Daisy was aghast and nervous, but faced up to the situation and the battery of press cameras.

One afternoon the Bishop of Norwich himself, complete in apron and gaiters, appeared at Hill House, to speak with Grandpa, who, as the Glebe tenant, had been acquainted with the Rector longer than most people. Grandpa remained loyal to the parson throughout. 'I speak as I find,' he said to the Bishop. 'I have known him a long time and I like the little gentleman.'

However, once the press had done their worst, there was nothing for it but a public defrocking, and the sad spectacle appeared in all the papers. So 'justice' was seen to be done. I shall not forget, nor forgive, that picture, the ignominy of it all. The

61

Church (I thought, as a teenager) was behaving in a most unseemly and unchristian way. Where was the forgiveness, the mercy, the help the Rector certainly needed just then? Instead, the treatment meted out to him by the Church and the public (for we were also to blame) simply drove the poor man to new excesses.

After the defrocking he was ostracized and unable to find work anywhere despite his talents. His wife and children left the Rectory. He intended to appeal, maintaining that the 'immorality' had never been proved, and many of us thought so too. He was always writing, writing up his case, but financing his defence was an expensive business and he resorted to some extraordinary fund-raising measures. Eventually, as everyone knows, he was to be found sitting in a cage full of lions at Skegness, where people paid sixpence to see 'Daniel in the lions' den'. Unfortunately, he didn't share Daniel's immunity; a few weeks later he was mauled by Freddie, one of the lions - more newspaper headlines - and died a few hours later in hospital. That was in 1937.

We were all dreadfully sad; he did not deserve this harsh fate. He was buried in his churchyard at Stiffkey, with great sorrow, and for many years people tended his grave and left bunches of fresh flowers. A rose bush still blooms there in the summer.

Grandpa Wordingham died a few months later in June 1938. He was 83.

Postscript

I left Norfolk in 1932 to take up an offer of a teacher training place at Avery Hill College in London. My forty-year career as a primary school teacher, first in London and later in Manchester (by which time I was married with two children) brought me into daily contact with young people, most of whom lived in deprived inner-city areas and had no experience of rural life. There were of course (and still are) poverty and hardship in the depths of the country-side, but there seemed to have been a richness of experience about my own childhood which contrasted sharply with that of many of the children I was teaching.

Holding on to my childhood memories has always been a source of inspiration for me. Now, as I look back at those early years of the last century from a world that could not be more different, I can see that despite the passage of time, in some ways my little corner of Norfolk is still recognisable in the essentials. Rural crafts may be competing with telecottages, village post offices with internet cafés, and you are more likely to come upon a Porsche than a pony-trap in the narrow lanes around Stiffkey. And yet the wide skies and the marshes and the ancient hedgerows are the same now as they always were. When I retired from teaching and returned to Norfolk in 1980 I knew I had come home.

**The author in her eightieth year with her daughter
at Hill House**